Rock-a-Bye

Babies and Woddlers

Teaching the Faith in the Nursery

Rock-a-Bye
Babies and Woddlers
Teaching the Faith in the Nursery

Beloved, we are God's children now.
(1 John 3:2a)

BY GLORIA JEAN FOSTER, EMILY STINSON, MELISSA STRAUSBAUGH, AND KERRY BLACKWOOD

All Scripture quotations, unless otherwise indicated, are from the New Revised Standard Version of the Bible, copyright 1989, Division of Christian Education of the National Council of the Churches of Christ in the United States of America. Used by permission. All rights reserved.

Scripture quotations marked (CEV) are from the Contemporary English Version © 1991, 1992, 1995 by American Bible Society, Used by Permission.

Every effort has been made to trace copyrights on the materials included in this publication. If any copyrighted material has nevertheless been included without permission and due acknowledgement, proper credit will be inserted in future printings after notice has been received.

www.abingdonpress.com

Photo Credits: Cover, pp. 11, 19, 20, 21, 29, 31, 33, 35, 36, 37, 48, 50, 51, 60-63: Jupiter Images

Photo Credits: pp. 4, 6, 10, 23-25, 27-29, 31-33, 35-37, 47, 49, 52: Design Pics, Inc.

Design and little teddy bear by Kay Meadows

09 10 11 12 13 14 15 16 17 18 — 10 9 8 7 6 5 4 3 2 1
Printed in the United States of America

Abingdon Press

TABLE OF CONTENTS

A Child

I am a child—a miracle to see.
Look at me and get a glimpse of what the future will be!

I cry loudly, I bang furiously, I giggle rapturously, I smile angelically.
I stare intently, I move quickly.

. . .

Please . . .
Hug me.
Hold me.
Talk to me.
Walk with me.
Feed me.
Play with me.
Sing to me.
Pray with me.

Teach me that the church can be
A loving, trusting place to be.

Through trust and love help me to see
that I am special and God loves me!

—MaryJane Pierce Norton

From *The First Three Years: A Guide for Ministry With Infants, Toddlers, and Two-Year-Olds*.
Used by permission of Discipleship Resources, © 1995.

A Special Message to Teachers, Leaders, and Caregivers

As a teacher in the infant room or nursery, you have the wonderful privilege of spending time with the youngest members of the family of faith as they form their first impressions of the church and begin their faith journeys. You also have the responsibility of relating to the parents and guardians of infants and woddlers as they entrust their children into your care while they are worshiping or participating in church activities. Teachers, leaders, and caregivers in the infant room or nursery are partners with parents or guardians in the Christian nurture of the children. For these parents or guardians, the infant room or nursery is the most important room in the church!

Jesus spent time during his ministry reaching out to people of all ages, including children. Infants and woddlers already belong to God. They do not have to become adults to be God's children—they were born God's children—as expressed in the Bible verse, "Beloved, we are God's children now" (1 John 3:2a). The way we care for each child with a cheerful smile, a kind word, and a gentle touch, along with the activities and messages of Scripture, song, and prayer that we share with the child, all work together to provide a nurturing environment and communicate the love of God. It is our purpose that these resources will be tools to help provide a nurturing, caring environment in the infant room or nursery.

The Rock-a-Bye series also includes "Toddlers and Twos." For children who move out of the babies and woddlers age group (birth through 18 months), their faith journeys can continue to be nurtured by using "Toddlers and Twos," which introduces them to specific Bible stories as well as more concrete learnings of the Christian faith.

Every teacher, leader, and caregiver who enters a church classroom where children are present is encouraged to spend moments in prayer before the session begins. You may wish to use the following prayer in your own preparation.

A Teacher's Prayer

Dear Loving God,

I thank you for the great privilege of serving in your church. I thank you for each family who will come to our church and especially for the infants and young children who will be a part of our classroom today. I pray for your guidance in all that I do and say to them. Help me to see each child with your eyes and to be an instrument to bring the blessings of your love into their lives, for I know that each child is a child of God.

Amen.

How to Use This Curriculum

This unique curriculum has been specially written for adults who teach and care for babies and woddlers (ages birth through eighteen months) in the church infant room or nursery. For these little ones, curriculum is everything the children experience from the time they enter the infant room or nursery until they are picked up. The purpose is to supply the tools needed to provide a quality ministry to these young children. Please look carefully at the sections on infants, their developmental characteristics, and curriculum ("What You Need to Know About Infants," page 8; "Give Them Love and Watch Them Grow," page 9; "What You Need to Know About Curriculum for Babies and Woddlers," pages 10-11). Pay special attention to the information on the developmental stages of these babies and how these stages impact their faith development.

Look at the ideas given, adapt them to your situation, and be ready to welcome these little ones and give them a good start toward becoming disciples of Jesus Christ.

Board Books

Recommended board books to use with this curriculum are: *God Loves Me, Jesus Is My Friend,* and *Church Is a Special Place.* These are available in Christian bookstores and through Abingdon Press. There are many times throughout a session in the nursery or infant room when these books can be read. Spend time holding a child in your lap, rocking the child, and reading the book. Even though the child will not be able to process all the information, he or she will begin to hear these simple words of faith.

Preparing the Room

Space is an important component of the curriculum. The infant room and/or nursery should be clean, neat, and bright. Place the poster from page 4 near the door so that it can be seen as parents or guardians enter the room.

The poster sets a good tone for what is to happen in the room. Design the room around the five discovery areas. There are posters provided for each area. Emphasized in each discovery area are: *Prayer, Promise, Praise,* and *Fingerplay.* Each poster has either a prayer, a Bible verse, a song, or a fingerplay to be used in that area. Four of the posters are available in the back of this Ministry Guide (pages 60-63), and all of them can be downloaded from http://Rock-A-Bye.AbingdonPress.com.

Activities

It is important that you interact with babies and woddlers, not just watch them. To guide this interaction, each area also has a page of teaching activities and suggestions designed to provide an experience that is faith-forming and appropriate to the stage of development. Following these teaching suggestions and activities will also keep the children safe and secure and help them develop the trust that is such an important lesson for infants and woddlers and an essential component of this curriculum.

FaithPoints

FaithPoints are provided for each area. These are basic concepts that will serve as the foundation for each child's faith development. The activities, songs, Bible verses, and prayers on the posters and in the teaching tips and activities will reinforce these FaithPoints with the child.

Spend lots of time talking, saying Bible verses, or reading to the babies. Even if you are saying the same thing over and over, babies learn from repetition. Soon they will begin to respond with their own "words."

Singing

Music is one of the most important ways a child learns. Do not worry about your voice quality, go ahead and sing! The songs in this resource use familiar tunes and are easy to sing. A baby will appreciate your vocal efforts even if you don't sound like a professionally trained singer.

Rock-a-Bye Lullabies and More is a CD to use with this resource. It is sold separately and is available in Christian bookstores. It can be used at any time in the infant room or nursery.

Posters

Posters are an integral part of this curriculum. Black-and-white images of four posters are included in the back of this book. Full-size color or black and white posters are available as a download from http://Rock-A-Bye.AbingdonPress.com. It would be preferable to laminate the posters or put them in a simple frame. You may download and print the posters yourself, or you may print them at a local print shop or photocopy shop.

Sample Forms and Letters

A section of sample forms and letters (pages 40-45) is included for help in keeping the necessary records and having needed information on each child. These forms can be used in a variety of ways and with a variety of people. They can be adapted as needed. Permission is given to photocopy them. Remember to keep all information updated and in a place easily accessible to the appropriate people.

Parent/Caregiver Messages

Included in this resource are Parent/Caregiver Messages (pages 47-59). All of these pages are reproducible. They are to be given to parents or guardians each month. Included in them are helpful bits of information, advice, and ideas to use with their babies and woddlers as they guide them into developing Christian faith. Make sure that every parent or guardian receives a page once a month.

Bibliography

Check the Bibliography (page 64) for a list of resources useful in providing a quality infant room or nursery ministry. One especially helpful resource is *The First Three Years,* published by Discipleship Resources. Pay close attention to *Safe Sanctuaries,* also published by Discipleship Resources, for information on providing a safe environment for children.

By Emily Stinson and Gloria Jean Foster

What You Need to Know About Infants

Infants (birth to one year):
- are totally dependent on others to meet their needs
- must have their physical needs met
- require love, care, and a safe environment
- like to look at new things
- develop language ability through crying, cooing, and babbling
- develop socially, cognitively, emotionally, and physically in an intertwined process

Infants learn when they:
- listen to music
- play with toys
- explore their environment and the objects in it
- look at pictures
- discover books
- relate to teachers, leaders, caregivers, and other children
- see, hear, touch, taste, and smell

Infants develop faith when they:
- receive love and nurturing care from parents and caregivers
- learn to trust adults, since trust is a foundation of faith
- have opportunities to express praise, joy, and thanksgiving
- learn that church is a happy and special place where people hear about Jesus and offer prayers to God
- see adults model their own spirituality

Give Them Love and Watch Them Grow

**Beloved, we are
God's children now.
(1 John 3:2a)**

The above Scripture tells us that we are all God's children—even the youngest people in God's world. Through them the Christian faith will continue. The babies and woddlers we care for will learn about and receive the love of God through those who care for them in the infant room and nursery. Developmental characteristics of babies and woddlers is provided; however, keep in mind that all children are unique and special and develop at their own speed.

Absorbers (5 to 8 Months)—Stage 3

- begin to sit unaided
- throw things, bang things, drop things, and enjoy playing this game with adults
- sometimes exhibit stranger anxiety
- enjoy watching what is happening around them
- mimic sounds
- understand names of familiar people and objects

Appropriate Practices:

- Introduce toys with different shapes.
- Link words to actions and objects.
- Provide space and places for infants to move freely.
- Frequently engage in games with babies who are interested and responsive.

Sleepyheads (Birth to 6 Weeks)—Stage 1

- show interest in voices
- can see, hear, feel, smell, and taste
- have cries that seem unconnected to specific meaning

Appropriate Practices:

- Hold babies close.
- Sing to babies while holding them.
- Provide things with bright colors to look at.
- Respond quickly to cries of distress.
- Engage in all interactions with gentle, supportive responses.
- Place babies on their backs to sleep.

Explorers (8 to 12 Months)—Stage 4

- respond to own name
- can say two or three words
- understand many more words
- move by scooting, crawling, and later walking
- begin teething with some associated misery
- pull themselves up to stand holding onto furniture
- try to build with blocks

Appropriate Practices:

- Provide safe spaces for babies to crawl, walk, and explore.
- Read to babies using lots of sounds.
- Talk to babies to help them learn words for their understanding and speaking.
- Repeat phrases such as "God loves you," "Jesus is your friend," and "Church is a special place."
- Use religious words, such as *God, Jesus, church,* and *Bible.*

Charmers (6 Weeks to 5 Months)—Stage 2

- begin to smile and laugh
- roll from back to tummy
- experiment with sounds
- start playing with hands
- have different cries for hunger, pain, fatigue
- begin to babble and coo

Appropriate Practices:

- Smile back at infants.
- Move babies from one place to another so that they can see different things.
- Imitate the sounds infants make.
- Talk and laugh with babies.

Woddlers (12 to 18 Months)—Stage 5

- scribble on large sheets of paper
- stack blocks
- stand without help
- walk alone without help but are "shaky"

Appropriate Practices:

- Provide large sheets of paper, crayons, and tables where woddlers can work.
- Provide uncluttered space for woddlers to crawl, stand, fall, and walk.

What You Need to Know About Curriculum for Babies and Woddlers

In the church infant room or nursery, the curriculum includes everything the child experiences. Resources, supplies, and equipment help the children grow in faith. *Rock-a-Bye Toddlers and Twos* is available for those children from nineteen months through thirty-six months.

Greeting the Parents or Guardians and the Babies and Woddlers

Talk to each child and parent or guardian as they arrive. Interact with the children as you take them. Have favorite toys handy to distract them. Many children will make the transition into the nursery or infant room easily. Around six to eight months, some infants begin to experience separation anxiety. Help the parents or guardians say good-bye, but if a child is having difficulty with separation, invite the parent or guardian to stay. If the parent or guardian leaves and the child is inconsolable, seek out the parent or guardian. An unfamiliar caregiver could be more than that child can handle on that day. Some churches require that all adults have a background security check before entering an infant room or nursery. Check with your church's safety policies.

Church Is a Happy Place

In caring for babies and woddlers, the most important thing we can do is provide a warm, nurturing environment that develops trust and mutual respect. As children learn that church is a trustworthy place and the adults there can be trusted to satisfy their needs, this becomes the basis for trusting God. As adults respond to the child's needs—to be fed, talked to, changed, played with—the child can see that *This person cares for me* and later *I know what it is like for God to care about me because I have experienced care from adults*. In the same manner, as a child learns that in church she or he is accepted and loved, then she or he will become ready to accept God's unconditional love and forgiveness.

Interaction With Adults

Adults in the infant room or nursery should always be interacting with the infants or woddlers, not talking with other adults. This helps children learn that they matter and that we enjoy helping them grow in faith.

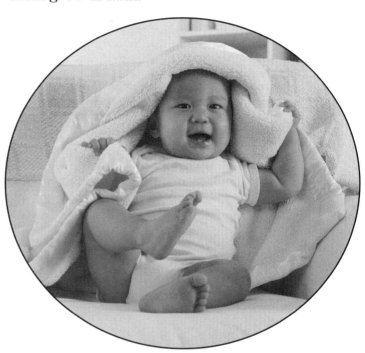

- Talk about God to the babies and woddlers. They recognize words they hear over and over. Use words that tell about God. Simple songs and prayers will help build the faith of a small child.

- Talk about the children. For the child, hearing "You are a child of God" and "God loves you" makes a connection between the child and God.

- Be sure to follow Christian practices in the church infant room or nursery. Always show love for every single child and adult.

- Play social games with babies and woddlers such as "Peek-a-Boo," "Hand It Over," or simple versions of "Hide and Seek."

Play

Play is the child's way of participating in the world. The nursery or infant room should have carefully chosen equipment, toys, and other materials that are of the appropriate size. The infant room is not the place for television-based toys or passive toys that do all of the action themselves. Instead, provide open-ended toys like blocks, dolls, vehicles, or toys the child can manipulate himself or herself.

Bounce chairs and wind-up swings are enjoyed by infants and are fine provided they are in these devices for short periods of time. Do not keep a child in one of these devices for an extended period of time. Babies also need floor time or "tummy time" to develop coordination.

Provide safe objects to look at, swipe at, and examine. Make the infant's world an interesting place.

Health and Safety

It is critical to babyproof the infant room or nursery and have basic security procedures in place. The most obvious safety factor is to stay *vigilant*. Watch the babies closely and never leave them unsupervised even for a moment. Here are some basic safety pointers, but do not limit yourself to these. Also see the section on security (page 14).

- Put safety plugs in all electrical outlets. Make sure no appliance cords dangle down where babies can pull on them. Use extension cords *very* sparingly.

- Put safety latches on low cabinet doors and drawers.

- Keep diaper pails covered and inaccessible to infants and woddlers.

- Make sure there are no small sharp objects around that could be swallowed, such as safety pins, staples, paper clips, hairpins, and so forth.

- Make sure toys are clean and in good repair and have no sharp edges.

- Clean toys regularly (at least once a month) with soap and water.

- Do not drink coffee or hot beverages around infants or woddlers. Check water temperature from hot water faucets and adjust downward if necessary.

- Never leave a child unattended on the changing table.

- Provide training in "Safe Sanctuaries" (see page 64) for all the people who work and volunteer in the infant room or nursery.

Again, the most important factor for safety is a caregiver who is thinking and watchful.

Experiences for Growing in the Faith

Babies and woddlers develop *faith foundations* as they interact with caring adults who help them experience trust in a safe space.

Infants and woddlers learn about the Bible and our faith traditions as they hear words and stories from the Bible and hear people talk about God, Jesus, the Bible, and prayer.

Babies and woddlers learn to relate to God and the church as they feel that the church is a good place to be, a place where people love and care for them.

By Emily Stinson

What You Need to Know About Room Setup

The infant room or nursery needs to be a healthy, safe place where infants and woddlers experience God's love and care. This may be the first place they come in contact with their church family, so it should be pleasant and comfortable for them and the parents or guardians. Space and furnishings should be appropriate for the children's physical, social, and spiritual needs.

Space
- Locate the nursery or infant room in a central area of the church easily accessible to parents or guardians. Provide good directional signs at each entrance.
- Allow space for parents or guardians to visit as they bring or pick up their children. (This can be outside of the room.)
- Arrange the entrance to limit the number of people who enter and leave the room.
- Rooms that are bright, clean, and neat are important for the children, parents, and teachers. The lighting should be bright to make the room more inviting.
- Control clutter and minimize things to stumble over.
- Provide a place for the children's belongings. Hooks or pegs can be mounted twelve inches apart on a board, or a cubicle can be provided for each child. Be sure *everything* is labeled.
- Include storage space for the room supplies (sheets, washcloths, changing supplies). If the storage is in low cupboards, add plastic door guards for the children's protection.
- Plan for safety. Make sure safety caps are in all electrical outlets within reach of crawling babies. Be prepared. Have emergency information and phone numbers posted as well as a first-aid kit and manual. There should also be an evacuation plan posted. See *The First Three Years* for sample nursery floor plans.

Furnishings
- Attach plastic unbreakable mirrors to the walls at a level where children in infant seats can see themselves.
- Rotate items in the room and on the walls.
- Arrange furnishings to give woddlers safe things to hold onto while learning to walk. These might make a low wall that can also serve as a divider to separate the play area from the sleeping area.

Rocking Area
Rocking chairs should be sturdy, comfortable, and stable with high backs and wide arms. They should be easy to get into and out of.

Diapering Area
The changing table should be sturdy with a washable surface that can be disinfected. Supplies should be easily accessible to adults but out of the reach of babies and woddlers.

Feeding Area
High chairs and/or small tables and chairs should be provided for the children to sit at while they eat. Arrange them so that the children can see one another.

Sleeping Area
Cribs should have appropriate safety features, including slats (2 $\frac{3}{8}$ inches apart), railing latches, proper mattress fit, and teething rails. They should be placed in a quiet area away from the play area and windows. Cribs should be about 2 feet apart.

Discovery Play Area
Provide an open space for crawlers to move. Place unbreakable, easy-to-clean toys on low bookshelves or in crates.

By Emily Stinson

Suggestions for Learning Through the Senses

SEE

Infants connect and respond most to facial expressions. The sight of something or someone familiar can create excitement for the child. Infants also begin life by seeing in black and white, but after the first two months, they start to view life in brilliant colors.

- Create and hang mobiles over cribs and the discovery play area. Objects that move and have bold contrasting colors help to stimulate visual development.
- Use hand-held mirrors or mount a mirror on a wall so that babies and woddlers can see and discover themselves and the world around them.
- Keep dolls in the classroom. Since babies and woddlers respond to facial expressions, dolls can provide a visual that they can study, recognize, and relate to.

SMELL

Infants have an innate ability to recognize the scent of their mothers from birth. The ability to smell often helps them to determine what is *safe* and *good*. Smells can both soothe and excite an infant.

- Place fresh fruit such as oranges in a basket and keep them in the classroom to provide a natural and inviting fragrance for children, parents, and teachers.
- Ask parents or caregivers to provide a cloth item with their scent on it, such as a pillowcase, a small blanket, or a T-shirt. Keep the item close to the child to create a calming sense that someone he or she loves is near.

TOUCH

Infants are natural-born explorers and learn about the world around them through the sense of touch, by using their fingers, bodies, and mouths.

- Keep *touch-and-feel* books in the room. Plastic, wipe-off books and books with textured pages provide babies and woddlers with an opportunity to stimulate their sense of touch and movement.
- Consider having a towel warmer in the infant room or nursery. This can be a perfect way to keep small blankets and cloths warm for swaddling and caring for the babies.
- Consider using a wipes warmer in the changing area. Keeping the infant relaxed and comfortable during the changing process can help to maintain a calming environment!

TASTE

Infants are born with a natural sweet tooth, due to the fact that breast milk is naturally sweet. It takes time for an infant's palate to adjust to new flavors. Provide them with a variety of textures to prepare them for learning to eat regular foods.

- Providing plastic, wipe-off books will allow babies and woddlers to use their mouths to explore as well as their hands. (Be sure to clean a book after each child plays with it.)
- Keep both smooth and textured teething rings handy in a refrigerator or freezer. The cool sensation often feels great on the gums and also allows babies and woddlers to taste and touch with their tongues.
- For caregivers concerned about choking, suggest *Baby Safe Feeders*™. This allows the child to try new foods and experience new textures of foods safely.

HEAR

Infants often associate comfort with sounds that they hear. They respond best to high-pitched sounds expressed through music and voices and sounds that mimic the womb.

- Consider purchasing a *womb-sounds* teddy bear for the room. These teddy bears contain recordings that mimic intrauterine sounds, which help to calm and soothe babies and even help them sleep. Another alternative is to purchase a *white noise machine*.
- Keep a music box handy. Babies and woddlers respond to pleasant and soft music. This can also stimulate the child's sense of hearing.

By Emily Stinson

Check-In and Security Options for Infant Rooms and Nurseries

Every parent or guardian who leaves a child in an infant room or nursery desires two things:

1. **A quick and easy check-in system.**
2. **A convenient mode for ensuring safety for the child, including a way to be contacted if needed.**

This page offers suggested tools for the check-in process and the security of our children.

Every church budget is different. This resource offers suggestions that allow churches to choose the security system that best fits their needs. (Disclaimer: None of the websites listed is directly endorsed by The United Methodist Publishing House.)

Check-In and Security Options

Sign-In Sheets
Reproducible sign-in sheets are available as part of this resource (page 40).

Check-In and Security Labels
www.churchnursery.com

Pager Systems (offering wired and wireless pagers, vibrating pager systems, and wireless classroom signal lights)
www.churchnursery.com
www.microframecorp.com
www.pager.net
www.jtech.com

Check-In Systems
www.excellerate.com
The Excellerate system provides each family with a keytag labeled with a barcode. The codes can be used with three different check-in options.

- **Express Mode:** A barcode scanner is set up at the check-in station and the parent or guardian scans the keytag of his or her child. The child's name badge and a check-in receipt are automatically printed, and no attendants are needed. In this mode, each child has an individual barcode number.

- **Touch-Screen Mode:** A touch-screen computer is left running at the check-in station. Each parent or guardian looks up her or his family (using last name or the last four digits of a phone number) and selects which child is checking in. A name badge and a check-in receipt print automatically. In this mode, each family has a single barcode but can select more than one child on the screen. No attendants are needed, and it is possible to set up a barcode scanner to simplify the process.

- **Attendant Mode:** A computer with keyboard and mouse is set up at the check-in station. An attendant asks the parent or guardian for last name or a partial phone number or scans the family's barcode. The attendant then selects which children are checking in that day.

www.lambslist.com
An attendant uses a computer to log on to the congregation's account at LambsList.com and looks up the family's information. Members can be located by first name, last name, or the last four digits of a phone number. The attendant selects which child or children are being checked in, and the system assigns a random security code to each child. The attendant can print labels with the child's name and code, one label for the child and one for the parent. The security code must be presented by the parent at pick-up time. Monthly and yearly subscriptions are available.

By Emily Stinson

Babies & Woddlers

Every Week in the Infant Room or Nursery

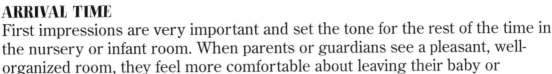

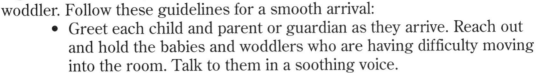

ARRIVAL TIME

First impressions are very important and set the tone for the rest of the time in the nursery or infant room. When parents or guardians see a pleasant, well-organized room, they feel more comfortable about leaving their baby or woddler. Follow these guidelines for a smooth arrival:

- Greet each child and parent or guardian as they arrive. Reach out and hold the babies and woddlers who are having difficulty moving into the room. Talk to them in a soothing voice.
- In many churches, parents, guardians, or caregivers can place infants and woddlers in cribs, infant chairs, or swings. Give the children toys to grab their interest.
- Have parents or guardians sign the children in using the forms provided for the room. Be sure all the information is up-to-date. Revise the information every three months.
- Collect the child's belongings and put these in the proper place. Label all the belongings as well as the child.
- Help the children and the parents or guardians deal with separation anxiety if this is an issue.

DURING THE HOUR

Move the children through the areas of the infant room or nursery as needed. Follow the teaching ideas and tips for each area.

PICK-UP TIME

- Be sure the person coming for the baby or woddler is authorized to take the child.
- Tell the parent or guardian what the child did during the hour. ("Look What _____ Did Today" on page 43.)
- Be sure the parent or guardian has all of the child's belongings.
- Invite the parent or guardian and the child back next week.
- Have the parent or guardian sign out.

Use arrival and pick-up times to introduce parents and guardians to one another if they do not know one another. Bulletin-board pictures can help parents or guardians know the other families who use the infant room or nursery.

By Emily Stinson

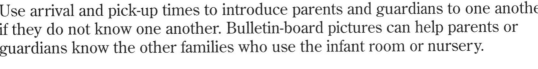

ORIENTATION FOR TEACHERS AND WORKERS

*Churches with several teachers and workers in the infant room or nursery
may wish to gather as a group for an orientation session.*

Before this session:
- *Make copies of the "Teaching Tips" and "Teaching the Faith" pages for each person.*
- *Download the posters from the website and have them printed and ready for hanging (http://Rock-A-Bye.AbingdonPress.com).*
- *Write the FaithPoints from page 18 on newsprint or a poster at the front of the room.*

PART 1

Devotional: Hold up the welcome poster (page 4) and read the poem.

Read "A Special Message to Teachers, Leaders, and Caregivers" (page 5).

Use "A Teacher's Prayer" (page 5). Discuss the importance of prayer in preparation for teaching.

Use "How to Use This Curriculum" (pages 6-7) as a guide to walking through the curriculum. This section will guide you in looking at the various pages of the curriculum. As each item is discussed, turn to the appropriate page to examine it more closely.

Read and discuss "What You Need to Know About Infants" on page 8 and "Give Them Love and Watch Them Grow" on page 9. As you read the developmental characteristics of each age level and stage, pause to think about specific children who may be in that stage now. Lift up the "Appropriate Practices" for each age level.

Turn to "What You Need to Know About Curriculum for Babies and Woddlers" (pages 10-11). Review the sections "Church Is a Happy Place," "Interaction With Adults," "Play," and "Experiences for Growing in the Faith."

Read the FaithPoints from the poster or newsprint.

Read "Preparing the Room" on page 6 and "What You Need to Know About Room Setup" (page 12) and think about the way your room is arranged in the different areas.

Turn to the welcome poster. Distribute the "Teaching Tips" pages to each person. Discuss how these can help teachers during the session as they move into the different areas of the room with the children. Also note the suggestions for learning through the senses (page 13).

Discuss a plan and a schedule for hanging the posters in the infant room or nursery.

Read the section on the discovery areas. Briefly look over the activities page for each of the five areas (pages 22, 26, 30, 34, and 38). Note that some of the activities are for particular ages or stages. Read an example of an activity related to a particular stage. (As time allows, examine activities from all the areas.)

Choose one area, such as the discovery play area. Look closely at the posters and activities and discuss how the FaithPoint shines through the activities and interaction with the children. (As time allows, have this discussion with activities and posters from all the areas.)

Practice singing the songs and doing the fingerplays from the posters and activities pages.

PART 2

(When preparing for this portion of the Orientation, please note the sample forms and parent letters found on pages 40-59 as well as the check-in and security options on page 14. Consider how these will be used in the ministry or if you have other items, policies, and procedures already in place that will need to be lifted up to the teachers and workers.)

Turn to "Every Week in the Infant Room or Nursery" (page 15) and discuss the procedures and practices that will be followed each week in the infant room or nursery for arrival and pick-up.

Spend detailed time discussing how to communicate with parents and guardians in the ministry with infants and woddlers, including such items as an information brochure for parents, the child information sheet, "What I Did Today" reports, injury reports, illness policies, and so forth.

Review and discuss the "Health and Safety" section in "What You Need to Know About Curriculum for Babies and Woddlers" (page 11).

Discuss any extra resources that are available for the infant room or nursery, such as books for adults and children (see the bibliography on page 64).

This session may also be a good time to review Safe Sanctuary policies and procedures.

By Gloria Jean Foster

Discovery Areas
in the Infant Room or Nursery

Faithpoints

ROCKING AREA

God Loves Me.

DIAPERING AREA

I Am a Child of God.

FEEDING AREA

God Takes Care of Me.

SLEEPING AREA

God Is Always With Me.

DISCOVERY PLAY AREA

God Helps Me Learn and Grow.

Teaching Tips and Posters for the Rocking Area

PRAYER

Recite prayers while rocking infants.
Prayers can be heard whether spoken aloud or as a quiet thought. Praying for an infant helps us to entrust the child into God's care.

PRAISE

Quietly sing "You Are Special" while rocking the baby or woddler.

Babies and woddlers typically respond to and actively seek out voices. Infants may respond by making eye contact or turning their heads toward music.

PROMISE

Recite Scripture verses to babies and woddlers while rocking them.
Reciting Scripture verses to a baby or woddler is an opportunity to share God's promises and is a reminder to us of God's faithfulness to fulfill them.

PLAY

Recite and demonstrate the fingerplay "Baby Grows."

Babies and woddlers respond to the rhyme and repetition of fingerplays. Using fingerplays reinforces the development of small motor skills.

PRAYER

Lord,
Thank you for this little one
given from above.
May your loving hands
work through mine
to show this child
your love.

PROMISE

"Beloved, we are God's children now." (1 John 3:2a)

PRAISE

You are special, you are special,
Child of God, child of God.
Love is all around you.
Love is all around you.
Child of God, child of God.
(Sing to the tune of "Are You Sleeping?")

PLAY

Baby Grows

Five little fingers on this hand.
(Hold up five fingers.)
Five little fingers on that hand.
(Hold up five fingers on the other hand.)
A dear little nose,
(Point to nose.)
A mouth like a rose,
(Point to mouth.)
Two little cheeks so tiny and fat.
(Point to cheeks.)
Two eyes and two ears,
(Point to eyes and then ears.)
And ten little toes,
(Point to toes.)
That's the way the baby grows.
(Author unknown)

teaching the Faith in the Rocking Chair

"Beloved, we are God's children now" (1 John 3:2a).

Where's Your Nose? (Stages 2, 3, 4)

Say: Where is *(child's name)***'s nose? There it is! There is** *(child's name)***'s nose.**
Then ask about the child's chin, ears, eyes, and fingers.
Say: God made you special. Let's thank God for making you special.

Read a Book to the Child (Stages 2, 3, 4, 5)

Choose books that are cloth, soft, or stiff board, since infants and woddlers will want to put them in their mouths. Hold the baby and let him or her look at the pictures. Point to objects or people on the pages, name the objects for the baby or woddler, and let the child begin to try to say the words. Use the board books available from Abingdon Press: *God Loves Me, Jesus Is My Friend,* and *Church Is a Special Place.*
Say: God gave us eyes to see things in books. Thank God for eyes.

Lullaby (Stages 1 and 2)

As you rock, sing this lullaby to the baby to the tune of "Twinkle, Twinkle, Little Star":
Rocking softly, sleepy babe,
Rest in Jesus' love for you.
Rocking gently, safely slumber,
Close your eyes and go to sleep.
Rocking softly, sleepy babe,
Rest in Jesus' love for you.
You can also sing other songs found on the "Rock-a-Bye Lullabies and More" CD.

See the Baby (Stages 3 and 4)

Use an unbreakable mirror and let the baby look at herself or himself. Point to the child in the mirror and **say: Who is this? Is this** *(child's name)***?**
Point out the child's nose while **saying: Is this** *(child's name)***'s nose?** Repeat with eyes and mouth.
Use the mirror to play peekaboo.
Then **say: God made all of you. Let's thank God for making you.**

Praise and Clap (Stages 2, 3, 4, 5)

Babies and woddlers love to clap their hands or have an adult gently clap with them if they have not learned that skill yet.
Sit with the baby or woddler on your lap and sing to the tune of "If You're Happy and You Know It":
If you're happy and you love God, clap your hands. *(clap, clap)*
If you're happy and you love God, clap your hands. *(clap, clap)*
If you're happy and you love God, then your hands will surely show it.
If you're happy and you love God, clap your hands. *(clap, clap)*
Repeat the song with the following verses, doing the different actions with the baby's hands:
Verse 2: **If you're happy and you love God, pat your legs.**
Verse 3: **If you're happy and you love God, tap your face.**
Verse 4: **If you're happy and you love God, stomp your feet.**

Babies & Woddlers

Teaching Tips and Posters for the Diapering Area

PRAYER

Recite prayers while changing infants.

Prayers can be heard whether spoken aloud or as a quiet thought. Praying for an infant helps us to entrust the child into God's care.

PROMISE

Recite Scripture verses to babies and woddlers while changing them.
Reciting Scripture verses to a baby or woddler is an opportunity to share God's promises to them.

PLAY

Recite and demonstrate "God Loves You."

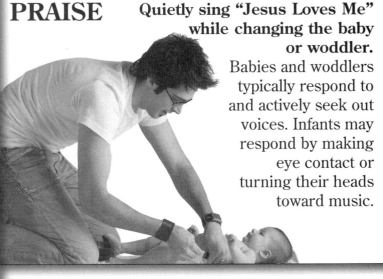

PRAISE

Quietly sing "Jesus Loves Me" while changing the baby or woddler.
Babies and woddlers typically respond to and actively seek out voices. Infants may respond by making eye contact or turning their heads toward music.

Babies and woddlers respond to the rhyme and repetition of play. Use fingerplays, toeplays, and tummy tickles to reinforce the development of small motor skills.

PRAYER

Dear God, So vulnerable this little one, trusting and carefree. Lord, let my life reflect the same. Humbly I ask, change me.

PROMISE

I praise you because of the wonderful way you created me. Everything you do is marvelous!

(Psalm 139:14, CEV)

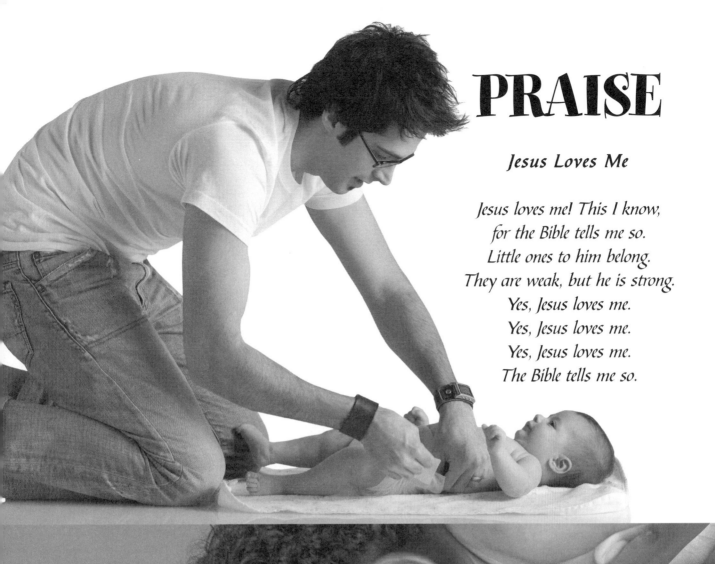

PRAISE

Jesus Loves Me

Jesus loves me! This I know,
for the Bible tells me so.
Little ones to him belong.
They are weak, but he is strong.
Yes, Jesus loves me.
Yes, Jesus loves me.
Yes, Jesus loves me.
The Bible tells me so.

PLAY

God Loves You

Here's a toe I love to wiggle.
(Wiggle one of the baby's toes.)
Here's a foot I love to jiggle.
(Wiggle the baby's foot.)
God loves you, Baby,
(or use baby's name);
(Gently cross the baby's heart
with the tips of your fingers.)
And so do I!
(Make a smiley face and tickle
the child's belly.)

teaching the Faith in the Diapering Area

Make a seashell mobile to hang over the changing table. Talk to the babies and woddlers as you change them.
Say: This shell came from the beach. God planned for all kinds of living things.

Make diapering or changing as pleasant as possible. Sing, talk, or provide a hand-held toy to occupy the baby or woddler.
Sing this song as the diaper is changed:

This is the way we change our diaper, change our diaper, change our diaper.
This is the way we change our diaper,
On a Sunday morning.

Another option is to sing "Jesus Loves Me."

Take advantage of diapering or changing time for easy, social interaction.
Lean over the baby or woddler and let him or her reach for your nose, grab your hair, and look into your face.

- Make the changing area convenient for the caregiver and safe for the child with none of the supplies within the baby's reach.
- Have the parents or guardians write diapering instructions with notes about lotions or powders.
- Change the baby or woddler when the child is wet or after a bowel movement. Check the child before feeding and within one half-hour of the parents' or guardians' arrival.
- When it is time for a change, have supplies ready before bringing the child to the changing area so the child will not be left alone.
- Check the parents' or guardians' instructions and get whatever is needed from the bag brought with the child.
- Be sure to have a baby wipe within reach. Get the clean diaper ready.
- Remove the soiled or wet diaper with a disposable glove. Move it out of the way and out of the child's reach.
- Put the dirty diaper in a pail with a secure lid.

Keeping the diaper-changing table clean for each child is very important to avoid spreading infections.

- Clean the diaper-changing area when the child is out of the area. First, take care of the soiled diaper. Cloth diapers need to be rinsed out in the toilet, then placed in a sealed plastic bag and put in the child's diaper bag. Disposable diapers should be placed in the garbage pail. Do not flush disposable diapers.
- Clean other supplies that were used and put lids back on lotions or ointments. Throw away any wipes or paper towels.
- Clean the diaper-changing table after each use with a solution of one-fourth cup of bleach to one gallon of water.
- If any toys were used while diapering, wash them and let them dry before giving them to another child.
- **Wash your hands after each diaper change. This prevents the spread of colds and other infections.**
- When a diaper has been changed, make a note on the "Look What _____ Did Today" form (page 43). When several parents show up at the same time to pick up their babies, you may not have time to tell them verbally.

Teaching Tips and Posters for the Feeding Area

PRAYER

Recite prayer while feeding the infant.

Prayers can be heard by God whether they are spoken aloud or as a quiet thought. Praying for a child helps us to entrust the child into God's care.

PRAISE

Quietly sing the song "Thank You, God" while feeding the infant. You can also sing along with the *Rock-a-Bye Lullabies and More* CD.

Infants respond to and actively seek out voices. Infants respond by making eye contact or turning their heads toward music and voices.

PROMISE

Recite Scripture verses to infants while feeding them.

Reciting Scripture to an infant is an opportunity to share God's promises and is a reminder to us of God's faithfulness to fulfill those promises.

PLAY

Recite and demonstrate "Sticky Snacks."

Babies and woddlers respond to the rhyme and repetition of play. Using fingerplays, toeplays, and tummy tickles reinforces the development of small motor skills.

PRAYER

Thank you, God, for snacks and treats,
for milk and juice and all I eat.
Thank you, God, for hands that feed
and care for me and all my needs.
Thank you, God, for helping me grow to
become BIG and STRONG and
WONDERFUL!

PROMISE

We give thanks to you, O God. (Psalm 75:1a)

PRAISE

Thank you, God
(Pray this prayer as the child drinks from a bottle or eats.)

Thank you for
the world so sweet.
Thank you for
the food we eat.
Thank you for
the birds that sing.
Thank you, God, for
everything.

PLAY

Sticky Snacks

Sticky fingers,
(Wiggle your fingers.)
Sticky toes,
(Wiggle child's toes.)
Sticky snacks
(Tap fingertips on thumb.)
Stuck on my nose.
(Point to nose.)
Wash my fingers.
(Rub hands together.)
Wash my toes.
(Wipe off child's toes.)
Clean me up, and
(Rub cheeks with hands.)
Watch me grow.
(Stretch arms high in the air.)

teaching the Faith in the Feeding Area

Being fed is the most important thing that happens in an infant's day. The baby is getting nourishment and nurturance. The holding, cuddling, and feeding contribute to the infant's and woddler's faith formation by helping develop some of the basic attitudes of trust and being cared for.

Be sure to communicate with parents or guardians about what the child can have to eat and drink. Follow their instructions carefully. (Make sure all bottles and other items are properly labeled with the child's name.)

Provide a place for mothers who are breastfeeding to feed their babies in comfort and privacy.

As you bottlefeed an infant (Stages 1-3), hold the infant in a secure position in the crook of your arm and close to your body. While you feed the infant, talk to him or her in a soothing voice with lots of repetition. Use the Prayer and Promise posters for a prayer and a Bible verse to say and the Praise poster for a song to sing. Play the *Rock-a-Bye Lullabies and More* CD and quietly sing along with it.

For woddlers who are able to eat finger snacks (Stages 4-5) include simple faith talk as you eat together. **Say: God has made so many good things to eat! Thank you, God, for juice, crackers, and raisins.**

Sing these songs in the Feeding Area:
(Tune: "The Farmer in the Dell")
**We thank you for our food,
We thank you for our food.
Thank you, God, for loving us.
We thank you for our food.**

(Tune: "Twinkle, Twinkle, Little Star")
**God is great. God is good.
Let us thank God for our food.
By God's hand, we are fed.
Give us, Lord, our daily bread.
God is great, God is good.
Let us thank God for our food!**
Sing along to "Praise Him, Praise Him" on the *Rock-a-Bye Lullabies and More* CD.

Teaching Tips and Posters
for the Sleeping Area

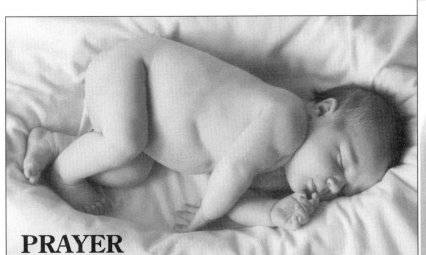

PRAYER
Recite prayers while the baby or woddler is asleep, playing, or standing in his or her crib.

Prayers can be heard by God whether they are spoken aloud or as a quiet thought. Praying for a baby or woddler helps us to entrust the child into God's care.

PLAY

Play "Dream Away."

Babies and woddlers respond to the rhyme and repetition of play. Fingerplays, toeplays, and tummy tickles reinforce the development of small motor skills.

PROMISE
Recite Scripture verses to infants while they are in their cribs.

Reciting Scripture to an infant is an opportunity to share God's promises and is a reminder to us of God's faithfulness to fulfill them.

PRAISE

Quietly sing the song "Sleepy Babe Lullaby" while the baby or woddler is in the crib.

Infants typically respond to and actively seek out adult voices. Infants might respond by making eye contact, turning their heads toward music or voices, or becoming relaxed and falling asleep.

PRAYER

When this busy little one finally rests his head
On the soft, warm blanket in his cozy bed,
While he nods off and dreams away,

Lie close beside to protect and pray.
As he sleeps I'm reminded of . . .
God grants sleep and everlasting love.

PROMISE

I can lie down and sleep soundly
because you, LORD, will keep me safe.
(Psalm 4:8 CEV)

PRAISE

Sleepy Babe Lullaby

Sing to the tune of "Twinkle, Twinkle, Little Star."

Rocking softly, sleepy babe,
Rest in Jesus' love for you.
Rocking gently, safely slumber,
Close your eyes, and go to sleep.
Rocking softly, sleepy babe.
Rest in Jesus' love for you.

PLAY

Dream Away

Sleepy baby, rest your head. *(Make praying hands and lay your face on hands.)*

Nestle in your cozy bed. *(Pretend to pull covers up and wiggle body downward.)*

Close your eyes and dream away. *(Point to eyes and close them.)*

When you awake, we'll laugh and play. *(Open eyes wide. Place hand over belly and giggle.)*

Until your peaceful sleep is done, *(Make praying hands again and lay face on hands.)*

Dream away, little one. *(Place index finger against lips and end fingerplay by saying, "shhh.")*

Teaching the Faith in the Sleeping Area

Sleep is very important to the growth of all babies and woddlers, especially those *sleepyheads* (birth to six weeks of age). The crib area should be placed in a quiet section of the room away from toy areas and equipment. Cribs should be at least 2 feet apart or have a sneeze barrier.

Mobiles are good to attach to cribs for babies who are going to sleep. Hang them approximately 12 inches from the baby's eyes and to one side of his or her head. Mobiles can be found at Christian bookstores or other outlets for baby products.

Stay with a baby who is going to sleep (Stages 1-3). You can sing lullabies such as the one on the Praise poster, repeat the Bible verse from the Promise poster, use the fingerplay from the Fingerplay poster, say the prayer from the Prayer poster, or play the *Rock-a-Bye Lullabies and More* CD. You might want to talk about the items on the mobile if the baby seems interested.

When the baby or woddler awakens, be sure to be there to make her or him feel secure. Hold the baby or woddler, talk softly to him or her, and do not forget to check and see if the child needs a clean diaper.

Speak in a soothing voice to a sleepy or fussy baby. Wait to be playful or animated until the baby or woddler is fully awake.

God is always with me.

Evaluate:

Think over the times when you have shared the Christian faith in the sleeping area. Did the babies and woddlers experience God's love?

Babies & Woddlers

Teaching Tips and Posters for the Discovery Play Area

PRAYER

Recite prayer while playing with the infant.
Prayers can be heard whether spoken aloud or as a quiet thought. Praying for an infant helps us to entrust the child into God's care.

PRAISE

Quietly sing the song "Eyes and Ears Praise" while playing with the baby or woddler.

Children typically respond to and actively seek out rhythmic voices. Infants may respond by making eye contact or turning their heads toward the music.

PROMISE

Recite Scripture verses to woddlers while they are playing.

Speaking Scripture to a woddler or a baby is an opportunity to share God's promises and is a reminder to all of us of God's faithfulness to fulfill those promises.

PLAY

Recite and demonstrate the fingerplay "The Itsy, Bitsy Spider."

Babies and woddlers respond to the rhyme and repetition of fingerplays. Fingerplays reinforce the development of small motor skills.

PRAYER

Praise to you, God,
for bubbles and rain, for balls
and blocks and peek-a-boo games.
Praise to you for my puzzles and books,
for snacks and foods my mommy cooks.
Praise to you, God, for creating me to
enjoy the wonder of all I see.
Amen.

PROMISE

Love one another. (John 13:34)

PRAISE

Eyes and Ears Praise
(to the tune of "London Bridge")

God gave you two EYES to see,
Eyes to see, eyes to see.
God gave you two eyes to see.
What do you see?
(Pause to talk about what you can see.)

God gave you two EARS to hear,
Ears to hear, ears to hear.
God gave you two ears to hear.
What do you hear?
(Pause to talk about what you hear.)

God gave you two HANDS to clap,
Hands to clap, hands to clap.
God gave you two hands to clap
your praise to God! (Guide the child in simple hand-clapping during this verse.)

God gave you a MOUTH to sing,
Mouth to sing, mouth to sing.
God gave you a mouth to sing
your thanks to God!
(Point to own mouth and help the child discover her or his mouth.)

PLAY

The Itsy, Bitsy Spider

The itsy, bitsy spider crawled up the water spout.
(Fingers crawl up arm.)
Down came the rain (Fingers crawl down the arm.)
And washed the spider out. (Throw arms to sides.)
Out came the sun and dried up all the rain.
(Raise arms above head and make a circle for the sun.)
And the itsy, bitsy spider crawled up the spout again. (Fingers crawl up arm again.)

teaching the Faith in the Discovery Play Area

The discovery play area should offer interesting objects for the baby or woddler to examine and explore. It should provide a feeling of comfort and security. This area also provides the baby with some of his or her first opportunities for socialization, leading to an understanding of what it means to live in a community of faith.

Use the plays from the posters (Stages 2-5).
Use these plays to interact with the child. Smile and help her or him repeat the actions as she or he is able.

Read to the child (Stages 2-5).
See pages 6, 13, and 22 for suggestions about choosing books and how to read to babies and woddlers.

Provide books for children at Stage 5 that they can look at and handle by themselves.

Sing with the children (All stages).
Use songs on the *Rock-a-Bye Lullabies and More* CD. Babies will enjoy hearing you sing and listening to the songs.

Talk with the child (All stages).
Use meaningful language and words such as *God*, *church*, and *love*.

Let the children experience the wonder of God's world (Stage 5).
Children can experience aspects of God's world such as water play with cups and funnels or placing figures in a sand tray. Stacking and knocking down blocks is another way the child experiences God's world.

Pass an object (Stages 3-5).
With the child sitting in front of you, hand him or her an object. **Say: Here you are.** Reach out, smile, and **say: Can you give it to me?** The child probably will, but if not, gently take it back, and **say: Thank you.** Repeat the game.

Play Ah, Boo (Stages 2 and 3).
This variation of *Peek-a-Boo* has been around for generations because babies respond so well to the game. Place the child on your lap facing you. Smile and **say: Ah, Boo, God loves you** or **Ah, Boo, God made you.** Repeat the game as long as the baby enjoys it.

Provide opportunities to practice new physical skills in a safe, open environment. Play a movement game (Stages 4-5). Say: God loves you, *(child's name)*. **Can you crawl to me?** Add other ways of moving, such as walking, as the child is able.

Babies & Woddlers

Sample Forms
& Letters

Sign-In Sheet

Today's Date _____

Child's Name _____

Child's Birthdate _____

Parent or Guardian Name _____

Location of Parent or Guardian _____

Today my child brought (circle all that apply):

     Bottle   Sippy Cup   Diaper Bag   Blanket   Toy   Snack

Check-In Time _____   Check-Out Time _____

Parent or Guardian Signature _____

Cut on this line--

Today's Date _____

Child's Name _____

Child's Birthdate _____

Parent or Guardian Name _____

Location of Parent or Guardian _____

Today my child brought (circle all that apply):

     Bottle   Sippy Cup   Diaper Bag   Blanket   Toy   Snack

Check-In Time _____   Check-Out Time _____

Parent or Guardian Signature _____

Babies & Woddlers

Child Information Sheet

Child's Name _____

Address _____

_____

Date of Birth _____

Name of Parent(s)/Primary Caregiver _____

Address _____

_____

Phone Numbers _____

Relationship to Child _____

_____

Feeding

Is your child breastfed or bottle-fed? _____

If breastfed, will the child accept a bottle? _____

Does your baby have any food allergies? _____

If so, list food allergies: _____

_____

Injury Report Form

Today's date _____   Time of injury _____

Injury report recorded by _____

Name of injured child _____

Age _____   Phone numbers _____

Address _____

_____

Parent/Guardian of child _____

Nature of accident (brief description) _____

_____

Nature of injury _____

_____

Immediate medical action taken _____

_____

Further medical attention needed _____

_____

INSURANCE INFORMATION (IF APPLICABLE):

Name of insurance company _____

Policy term _____

Agent _____   Group number _____

Signature of report preparer _____

As the parent or guardian of the injured child, I have reviewed and understand the
information given in this report.
Signature of parent or guardian _____

Look What .... Did Today!

Sleeping

_____ I Napped   _____ No Nap

From _____   To _____

From _____   To _____

From _____   To _____

Rocking

Held and lovingly rocked by:

_____

_____

_____ We sang a song.

_____ We said a prayer.

_____ We shared a Scripture.

_____ We played.

Diapering

My diaper was changed at:

_____ A.M./P.M.
_____ Wet   _____ Dry   _____ BM

_____ A.M./P.M.
_____ Wet   _____ Dry   _____ BM

_____ A.M./P.M.
_____ Wet   _____ Dry   _____ BM

Playing

I enjoyed playing with:
_____ blocks
_____ puzzles
_____ puppets
_____ push/riding toys
_____ musical instruments
_____ swing/bouncy seat
_____ books

Feeding

_____ Mom fed me herself.

_____ I was given a bottle.

_____ oz. at _____

_____ oz. at _____

_____ oz. at _____

Feeling

Today I was feeling:
_____ happy   _____ fussy
_____ content   _____ sick
_____ playful   _____ sad
_____ hungry   _____ sleepy
_____ shy   _____ angry

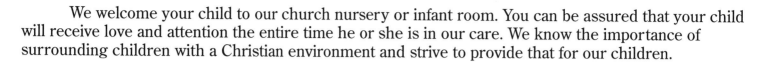

Welcome to Our Infant Room/Nursery

We welcome your child to our church nursery or infant room. You can be assured that your child will receive love and attention the entire time he or she is in our care. We know the importance of surrounding children with a Christian environment and strive to provide that for our children.

Our infant room/nursery is staffed by

_____

_____

Procedures

First-Timers
If this is your child's first time, please complete the Child Information Sheet provided by the childcare workers. Please include any information about allergies or other conditions or special instructions. This will help us to get to know your child and his or her individual needs.

What to Bring
Please bring a sufficient supply of items needed such as bottles, diapers, extra clothing, or a favorite toy. For those being potty-trained, please bring pull-ups. Please make sure all items brought with the child (diaper bag, bottle, pacifier, toys, and so forth) are labeled with the child's name.

Check In
Each time you bring your child to the nursery or infant room, please follow the check-in procedures provided by the staff and provide appropriate information about where you will be (for example, 9:45 in Sunday school in Room #_____ and 11:00 in worship) as well as your name or the name of the person who will be picking up the child.

Nametag
Please place a nametag on the back of your child. Also mention any allergies such as wheat, dairy, and so on. We use identification stickers to ensure her or his safety.

Dropping Off and Picking Up Your Child
For your child's safety, we ask that only adult family members drop off and pick up children.

Babies & Woddlers

Welcome to Our Infant Room/Nursery

Illness

Please do not bring your child into the infant room or nursery if he or she exhibits any symptoms of illness, including:

- fever above 98.6° F
- vomiting
- diarrhea
- discharge from ears or eyes
- cloudy or thick runny nose
- rash associated with viral or bacterial infection
- cold or sore throat
- contagious illness (chicken pox, pinkeye, and so forth)
- any major physical discomfort within the past 24 hours

Suggestions for Dealing With Separation Anxiety

Most young infants make a smooth transition into the nursery or infant room. However, some babies experience separation anxiety at about six to eight months of age. This is a healthy, natural part of growth and simply means that your baby loves you and wants to be with you and feels secure with you. Trust has developed between you. However, if a child becomes upset as you are leaving, the separation can be difficult.

Arrive early enough to allow time for a routine: signing in, placing the child's belongings in the space provided, saying goodbye. Greet the caregivers warmly and cheerfully. Let the caregivers help with goodbyes as they hold the child and begin to relate to the child. Remind the caregivers of your child's favorite toys and activities. Let your baby know that you like and trust the caregivers.

Questions?

If you have questions about the Infant Room or Nursery, please contact:

_____

_____

Parent or Caregiver Messages

the following pages are to be photocopied and sent home once a month
with the children.
they are to be used to share the Christian faith at home
with babies and woddlers.

PARENT/CAREGIVER MESSAGE
SEPTEMBER
"Praise the LORD!" (Psalm 117:2c)
FAITH WORD: *GOD*

A Message of Hope for Those Who Love and Care for Babies . . .

You have been given a child to love and care for. Now comes the daunting task of raising the small wonder entrusted to your care. Bringing the child to church is the beginning of a spiritual journey for both you and your child. Your fortunate child is going to hear about **God, Jesus, the Holy Spirit, Love, Peace, Joy, Hope, Faith, Church,** and so much more. Today is just the beginning! Spend time this week sharing faith words and small faith sentences with your child. Repeat these words and sentences while you feed the baby, diaper the baby, and rock the baby. Perhaps you have wondered what to do or say in these situations. Saying these words and sentences helps convey to the infant the love God has for her or him and the love you have for her or him. **Repeat these words often:**

God

Jesus

Holy Spirit

Love

Peace

Joy

Hope

Faith

Church

Repeat these faith sentences over and over to your child:

God loves you, *(child's name)*.
Jesus is your friend, *(child's name)*.
I love you, *(child's name)*.
God's peace is with you, *(child's name)*.
You bring joy to my life, *(child's name)*.
(Child's name), God gives us hope when we are sad.
Have faith in God, *(child's name)*, and your life will be blessed.
(Child's name), the church is a special place where we learn about God and Jesus.

PARENT/CAREGIVER MESSAGE
OCTOBER

"God saw everything that he had made, and indeed, it was very good."
(Genesis 1:31)
FAITH WORDS: *GOD* and *GOOD*

God has created a good and colorful world that we can enjoy.

During the month of October, there is beauty in many places in the world. The leaves are changing, and their colors are vibrant. Even though your small baby will not be able to tell you what colors the leaves are, you can tell your child about them.

Say to your child: The leaves on the trees are changing colors. (Hold your baby and point to a tree changing color.) *God* **has made a beautiful world. Everything** *God* **makes is** *good,* **including you.**

If possible, spend time outside with your infant. Put the baby in a stroller and walk around the block, to a park, to a store, around the outside of a mall, on paved walkways, and so forth. Most children enjoy movement. Point out nature to the child, such as colorful leaves, clouds in the sky, the sun, the sunset, birds, and fall flowers. **Say:** *God* **made all these things, and they are** *good.* Repeat the Bible verse over and over again to the child. **Say:** *God* **saw everything that he had made, and indeed, it was very** *good* (Genesis 1:31). Talk to your child while changing the child, feeding the child, dressing the child, or getting the child in and out of the car seat. He or she will enjoy the conversation.

Experience These October Activities With Your Child:

1.   Visit a pumpkin patch with your child. Hold her or his little fingers out to touch a pumpkin. As the child touches the pumpkin, **say: the pumpkin is smooth and orange.** *God* **made pumpkins. Everything** *God* **made is** *good.*

2.   Do this fingerplay with your baby:
Say: The pumpkin is round and big. *(Form a big pumpkin with fingers touching each other in a big circle.)*
My fingers are short and small. *(Open and close baby's fingers.)*
God **made everything,** *(Make a big circle with arms.)*
Pumpkins and all.

3.   Give your child a hug and **say: I love you, my little pumpkin!** *God* **made you, and you are** *good!*

Babies & Woddlers

PARENT/CAREGIVER MESSAGE
NOVEMBER
"I will thank you forever." (Psalm 52:9)
FAITH WORD: *THANKFUL*

Learning to Be Thankful

Learning to be *thankful* for what we have is a lesson all of us need. As you raise this precious baby of yours, you will probably have to explain the difference between wants and needs. This month is a time to be *thankful* to God for all we have. Practice *thankfulness*, and express *thankfulness* to your child and in front of your child. Begin by *thanking* God for the many blessings in your life. In your child's hearing, **repeat these phrases or similar ones:**
Thank **you, God, for the rain today.**
Thank **you, God, that we have food to eat.**
Thank **you, God, for a home to live in.**
Thank **you, God, for our family.**

Other activities to teach *thankfulness* include:

1. **Repeat the Bible verse at least once a day to your child: "I will thank you forever" (Psalm 52:9).**

2. Hold a soft toy in front of your baby (for babies about four months old), moving the toy in front of the baby's eyes. Let the child track the toy with his or her eyes. If the child is capable of reaching for and grabbing the toy, allow the child to do so. **Say:** *Thank* **you, God, that** *(child's name)* **can play this game with me. I love** *(child's name)* **and I know you do, too. Amen.**

3. November is a month when we particularly remember the food we have been given. If your baby is old enough to eat a banana, enjoy a banana snack with your child. Say: I am *thankful* we have bananas. God is good to give us bananas to eat.

4. Here is a simple faceplay to use with babies, especially those from four months to twelve months who are becoming very interested in learning their facial parts:
Here is my nose to smell my food. *(Point to baby's nose.)*
Here are my eyes to see my food. *(Point to baby's eyes.)*
Here is my mouth to eat my food. *(Point to baby's mouth.)*
Here is my tummy that likes God's good food! *(Rub baby's tummy.)*

5. Thanksgiving would not be the same without turkey fingerplays with babies and young children. **Repeat this Thanksgiving fingerplay with your child:**
(Hold up baby's fingers one by one.)
There was one little turkey with nothing to do. He invited a friend, and then there were two.
Two little turkeys standing by a tree, she invited a friend, and then there were three.
Three little turkeys standing at the door. One invited a friend, and then there were four!
Four little turkeys all juicy and fat. Thank goodness for turkeys— they're a good snack!

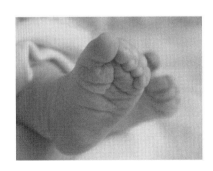

PARENT/CAREGIVER MESSAGE
DECEMBER
"And you will name him Jesus." (Luke 1:31b)
FAITH WORD: *JESUS*

The Gift of a Baby

Jesus was the first Christmas gift, and he came as a baby. This might be your first Christmas with your baby. Cherish every minute of it. Before long, you may be busy making angel's wings and finding a bathrobe for a shepherd's costume. This Christmas, share the love and tenderness of the season with your baby. There are many ways to share the love and warmth you feel for your baby just as Mary and Joseph felt for *Jesus*.

Rocking, Storytelling, and Singing

Even though your child is very small, you can begin to tell the Christmas story to him or her. When he or she is calm and relaxed, rock your baby and **tell the story from long ago:**

Many years ago in a small town called Bethlehem, there was a little baby boy born whose name was *Jesus*. His mother's name was Mary. She wrapped him and kept him warm. Mary rocked him and sang to him. Mary loved him just as I love you. God loved *Jesus*, just as God loves you.

Sing "Away in a Manger," "Silent Night," or some of the lullaby songs on the *Rock-a-Bye Lullabies and More* CD. Make a commitment to spend at least four quiet moments during the month of December rocking, cuddling, and singing with your baby.

A Nativity Set

For the next few years, an important part of your Christmas decorations should be an unbreakable nativity set. They are available in cloth, plastic, or wood. They don't have to be great works of art. They need to be nativity sets that the children can touch and move around and use to tell and retell the Christmas story. You will enjoy watching and listening to your child learn the story in more detail as she or he grows.

An Active Game

Another game that babies love to play is "Clippity-Clop."

Clippity-clop, clippity-clop. *(Pat hands on lap.)*
Joseph brought the donkey to Mary.
Clippity-clop, clippity-clop. *(Pat hands on lap.)*
Mary put the things they needed for their trip on the donkey.
Clippity-clop, clippity-clop. *(Pat hands on lap.)*
Mary, Joseph, and the donkey walked down the road to Bethlehem.
Clippity-clop, clippity-clop. *(Pat hands on lap.)*
Mary and Joseph were ready for *Jesus*.

PARENT/CAREGIVER MESSAGE
DECEMBER
"And you will name him Jesus." (Luke 1:31b)
FAITH WORD: *JESUS*

Decorating the Christmas Tree

If you decorate your home with a Christmas tree, this is a wonderful and exciting time for your baby. If you have a child with allergies or asthma, put up an artificial tree since fir trees create problems for people with allergies.

Babies will enjoy watching the shiny and colorful ornaments hanging on the tree limbs. If the child is capable of standing and walking, small or breakable ornaments should never be hung on lower branches.

While the tree is being decorated, play Christmas music and sing along with it. The baby will enjoy the audio and visual stimulation. And the baby will not be critical of your singing!

Toys Are Not Necessary!

Despite our material-crazed culture, your baby does not care if he or she receives any Christmas presents! What a relief! What he or she needs from you **this** Christmas is to celebrate by learning, in a very simple way, the birth of the Christ child; by playing Christmas games; by touching, feeling, and playing with an unbreakable nativity set; by decorating a Christmas tree; and by being rocked and sung to just as *Jesus* might have been by his parents. Make this Advent and Christmas season a time in your home to relax, be warm, and share love with family members.

Keep in mind the faith word for the month: *Jesus.* It can be repeated often when you **speak the Bible verse several times a week to your child: "And you will name him Jesus" (Luke 1:31b).**

PARENT/CAREGIVER MESSAGE
JANUARY
"Greet one another with a holy kiss." (1 Corinthians 16:20b)
FAITH WORD: *LOVE*

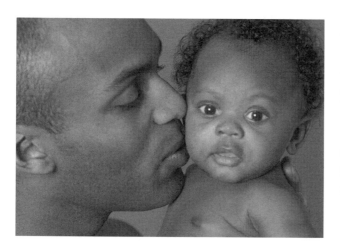

Greeting Your Baby or Woddler Warmly in Love

During the cold, winter month of January, practice warmth in your family. Every time you pick up your baby or woddler from the crib, the daycare, the church nursery, or the babysitter's, practice greeting the child warmly in *loving* ways. If you use this practice in just these four situations, you will discover joy in your baby's eyes when he or she sees you; and you will feel the same joy wash over you. Greet your baby or woddler with a kiss as the Scripture says (1 Corinthians 16:20). Use these following words to **greet your child:**

Hello, *(child's name)*, **I am so glad to see you. It has been a long night, and I have missed you.**

Peace be with you, *(child's name)*. **I** *love* **you and God** *loves* **you.**

(Child's name), **did you have a good day today?**
(Child's name), **God has been with you while you were here. I hope you felt God's presence with you.**

Develop your own words of greeting specifically for your child. Don't hesitate to also use words of humor when you greet your child. *Faith doesn't always have to be serious!*

Teach the Song "Jesus Loves Me"

Many of us have happy memories of learning to sing this song, which is the first song many of us learn about our faith. Even woddlers can begin to sing some of the words in some of the correct places. It is enough that babies and woddlers hear these words of *love* and incorporate these words of faith into their brains and hearts. **Sing this song while cuddling your child, strolling with your child, or caring for your child:**

Jesus loves me! This I know, for the Bible tells me so.
Little ones to him belong; they are weak, but he is strong.

Yes, Jesus loves me! Yes, Jesus loves me! Yes, Jesus loves me! The Bible tells me so.
Words by Anna B. Warner, 1860.

Babies & Woddlers

PARENT/CAREGIVER MESSAGE
FEBRUARY
"Love one another."
(John 13:34a)
FAITH WORD: *LOVE*

The Faith Word This Month Is Love!

It would be impossible for the faith word this month to be anything other than *love*. And while you will be telling your baby or woddler many times this month that you *love* her or him, do not forget to **repeat the Bible verse to your child: "Love one another" (John 13:34a).** If possible, repeat the Bible verse every time you feed your child. The child will hear these words of faith and process them in his or her brain, and faith will become foundational in the child's life.

Other Ways to Share Love

1. If your child is old enough to chew cookies, make or buy very plain heart-shaped cookies. Never give a young child cookies containing food items that might choke a child or that the child might be allergic to, such as nuts or hard candies. All food must be soft and chewable! When giving your woddler the cookie, **say: Hearts remind us that God *loves* us, Jesus *loves* us, and we can *love* one another.** If there are preschool children in your family as well as woddlers, they will also enjoy this activity.

2. If you live in an area where there is snow, and it is not too cold, take your baby or woddler outside and make a large heart in the snow with a stick. **Say: Hearts remind us that God *loves* us, Jesus *loves* us, and we can *love* one another.**

3. Decorate the home nursery. Hearts are very simple to make. They can be made by folding pieces of red or pink construction paper in half, drawing a half-heart on the fold of the construction paper, and then cutting it out. Decorate your baby's nursery with hearts. Put heart stickers inside the hearts. Every time you pick up your baby or woddler from naptime, remind him or her of the symbol of the heart. **Say: Hearts remind us that God *loves* us, Jesus *loves* us, and we can *love* one another. I especially *love* you, (child's name).** In yet another way, your child has experienced the *love* of God through you! Continue to pray each day for God to use you as an instrument of peace and *love* for your child. God will honor your request.

Have a happy month filled with *love*!

PARENT/CAREGIVER MESSAGE
MARCH

"[Love] bears all things, believes all things, hopes all things, endures all things." (1 Corinthians 13:7)

FAITH WORD: *HOPE*

Hope comes in the spring.

By March, many parents and caregivers of babies and woddlers are feeling very "cooped up." It has been a long winter, and you need *hope* for the coming spring. Spring will come. It won't be long before new grass sprouts up and birds sing. But until spring arrives, concentrate on prayer. Prayer can help parents and caregivers survive any storm they experience as they raise their children. Not only can you pray, but it is not too early to help your child learn to pray.

Teach your older baby or woddler the following fingerplay to prepare for prayer:

Open wide and shut real tight, open wide and shut real tight. (*Open fingers wide and then close into a fist. Repeat.*) **Put my hands away.** (*Put hands in lap.*) **Now it's time to pray.** (*Fold hands together as for prayer.*) **Pray: Thank you, God, for the spring we are *hoping* and waiting for. Amen.**

Tell your child that Jesus taught people how to pray. **Say: When we pray, we *hope* and we believe that God is with us.** Show your child a picture of Jesus. Put it in a place where your child can see it daily. Point to the picture and **say: This is Jesus, who loves you. Amen.**

Illustration by Nancy Munger from *Jesus Is My Friend,* © 2009 Abingdon Press.

Babies & Woddlers

PARENT/CAREGIVER MESSAGE
APRIL

"Clap your hands, all you peoples; shout to God with loud songs of joy." (Psalm 47:1)

FAITH WORD: *JOY*

This Bible verse tells us to clap and be *joyful*. When we shout to God, we can shout with loud songs of *joy*.

This is a *joyful* time of year when new life takes over the earth. We also celebrate the new life all of us have in Jesus Christ.

Your young child is often *joyful* on her or his own. Nothing compares to that wide, toothless smile when she or he sees you. Spend some time being *joyful* with your child. Sing happy songs, pantomime them with your child watching, and move your child's hands as you sing the songs. Some songs to sing with your child are:

(Sing to the tune of "Row, Row, Row Your Boat.")
Joy, joy, joy I have, *joy* within my heart.
Joy, joy, joy I have, *joy* within my heart.

(Sing to the tune of "London Bridge.")
I have *joy* within my heart, in my heart, in my heart.
I have *joy* within my heart.
I love Jesus.

You can sing "If You're Happy" from the *Rock-a-Bye Lullabies and More* CD (available from Christian bookstores).

These are simple songs using common tunes. Whatever you sing, *be joyful!*

As soon as most children are old enough to be fairly steady on their feet (12-18 months), they will bounce to music. This is always a delightful sight. Encourage your baby and woddler to do this by playing *joyful* music. You can buy the *Rock-a-Bye Lullabies and More* CD and play it at home and in the car. Let your baby or woddler become familiar with songs of faith. As soon as his or her verbal abilities mature, he or she will sing along with the music. Sing with your child. Your child will enjoy hearing your familiar voice.

You Can Tell the Easter Story!

Even though a young baby will not be able to understand the meaning of the Easter story, you can help them become familiar with it. Hold your baby in your arms to play this Easter game. Walk to an empty box with your baby and **say: Let's pretend to be Mary. We will walk to see Jesus.** *(Look inside the box.)* **Jesus is not in here! Jesus is alive! Let's go tell others that Jesus is alive!** *(Run gently away from the box to tell others that Jesus is alive!)*

Take an Early Spring Walk

This is also the time of year to take your baby outside and point out all the wonderful nature that is popping up all over the earth! The walk will be good for both of you.

PARENT/CAREGIVER MESSAGE

MAY

Beloved, we are God's children now.

(1 John 3:2a)

FAITH WORD: *FAITH*

Your baby or woddler is already a child of God.

Babies and woddlers belong to God. They are "children of God" now. If your child is a woddler, he or she might have heard the name "Jesus" before. Now is the beginning of your child's Christian *faith.* You can tell your child that Jesus is God's Son and that we can have *faith* in Jesus and in God. The more your child hears these affirmations of *faith,* the more your child will believe in them. An exciting concept for small children to learn is that Jesus was small, just like they are.

Enjoy playing this game with your woddler. If your baby is too small to make these body movements, she or he will enjoy watching you make them and will laugh at you (four months and older)!

Little Jesus, asleep in your bed. You sleep in your bed all day long. *(Lie down on the floor.)*

Soon you will be sitting up straight and tall. *(Sit up straight.)*

And then you will learn to crawl. *(Crawl around.)*

Next you will learn to stand up tall. *(Stand up.)*

Soon you will take steps, one and two. *(Take two steps.)*

Soon you'll be walking all around, just as grownups do. *(Walk in place.)*

Babies also enjoy learning their body parts. A small baby will smile and chuckle when you point out and gently touch parts of his or her face and body. **This is your sweet little nose. I love you completely from your head to your toes.** *(Touch the baby's nose and wiggle the baby's toes.)*

These are your pretty little eyes. This is your sturdy little chin. *(Point to the baby's eyes and touch the baby's chin.)*

I love you completely—all that is without and all that is within. *(Cuddle the baby closely.)*

Illustration by Nancy Munger from *Jesus Is My Friend,* © 2009 Abingdon Press.

Babies & Woddlers

PARENT/CAREGIVER MESSAGE

JUNE

"And the disciples were filled with joy and with the Holy Spirit."
(Acts 13:52)

FAITH WORDS: *JOY* and *CHURCH*

Sing this song of *joy* to your baby or woddler to the tune of "She'll Be Coming 'Round the Mountain":

O-o make a *joyful* noise unto the Lord.
O-o make a *joyful* noise unto the Lord.
O let's worship God with gladness,
O let's worship God with gladness.
O-o make a *joyful* noise unto the Lord.

(Based on Psalm 100:1. Words: Daphna Flegal and Sharilyn S. Adair. © 1997 Abingdon Press.)

At about six months old, babies begin to enjoy fingerplays. Although they will not be coordinated enough to play them exactly like you do, they will be fascinated watching you do them and will enjoy having you hold their little hands and fingers to make the fingerplay motions. (Of course, singing to babies and infants is always encouraged. We have included the above song for that reason.) One of the oldest and best-loved fingerplays for babies is the following:

Here is the church. (*Put hands together and intertwine the fingers between the palms.*)

Here is the steeple. (*Put up the forefingers together to form a steeple.*)

Open the doors, (*Separate the thumbs to reveal the intertwined fingers.*)

And see all the people! (*Move the intertwined fingers. They are the people!*)

Going to *church* every Sunday should become a family habit. It is important that babies and woddlers recognize that *church* is a special and happy place where they will learn about God and Jesus. Hopefully, they will be filled with *joy* while they are there. Your positive attitude toward *church* will influence your child tremendously. Talk about *church* in a positive way.

Walk around the *church* holding your baby or woddler and pointing out the Christian symbols. If you are familiar with what the symbols mean, explain them to your child. Although the child will not understand the significance of the symbols, she or he will begin to understand that the symbols are important and remind us of what we believe.

Read *Church Is a Special Place,* © 2009 Abingdon Press. (Look for it in Christian bookstores.) This book explores what children will see and experience when they go to *church*. Children will begin to understand that *church* is a special place filled with special people!

Another activity to enhance your woddler's growing love and appreciation of *church* is to let her or him create a scribble banner. A child who is twelve months old or older can participate in this activity. Give him or her a large piece of white paper and crayons under your watchful eyes. Turn on the *Rock-a-Bye Lullabies and More* CD. **Say: We can listen to music about God and *church* and Jesus. The music fills our hearts with *joy*. We can create a pretty banner that shows how much we love God.**

Hang the banner in your home. Point to it frequently with your child. **Say: The banner reminds us that God is with us and loves us.**

PARENT/CAREGIVER MESSAGE
JULY
"Peace to this house!" (Luke 10:5b)
FAITH WORD: *PEACE*

Prayer and Reciting Scripture Are Avenues to Peace.

Creating *peace* in your home allows your child the freedom to discover God. One way to establish *peace* in any home is through prayer. As a parent or caregiver, you can pray for the people in your home in several ways and at numerous times during the day. It is wise to establish a prayer time every day. Praying before meals is also a good practice.

Let your child hear your prayers. Pray out loud and as often as you can. Pray in situations when your child is with you, such as when you are driving, folding laundry, or making dinner. Your child will begin to understand that prayer is important to you. Hold your infant and pray with the infant in your arms. **Pray: God bless this child and all who come into her life today. Give them *peace*, patience, and love.**

Recite Scripture and prayers when you feed your child, change your child, dress your child, and put your child to sleep. A soothing voice and a prayer will help a child become *peaceful*.

Hold your baby in your arms and thank God for your child. **Pray: Thank you, God, for** *(child's name)*. **Thank you for his eyes, his nose, and his toes. Help him to grow and to be a *peaceful* person. Amen.**

Using Scripture as You Pray

Reciting Scripture while holding your baby or woddler will soothe the child and help her or him hear words of faith. (It will soothe you, also.)

Recite Psalm 23:1-3

"The LORD is my shepherd, I shall not want.
He makes me like down in green pastures;
he leads me beside still waters;
he restores my soul.
He leads me in right paths
for his name's sake."

Recite Matthew 19:14

"Let the little children come to me, and do not stop them; for it is to such as these that the kingdom of heaven belongs."

Recite 1 John 4:16b

"God is love, and those who abide in love abide in God, and God abides in them."

Before feeding your baby in the high chair, **recite this prayer with your baby or woddler:**
**Thank you, God, for this food.
Let it help** *(child's name)* **to grow and share your love and *peace* with everyone she meets. Amen.**

PARENT/CAREGIVER MESSAGE
AUGUST

"And he [Jesus] took them up in his arms, laid his hands on them, and blessed them." (Mark 10:16)

FAITH WORD: *JESUS*

Your child can begin to hear the faith word *Jesus*. You can talk about *Jesus* by telling your child that *Jesus* is God's Son and *Jesus* loves him or her. Provide songs and games in which *Jesus'* love for your child is emphasized. Sing this song to your child to the tune of "Mary Had a Little Lamb":

**Jesus loves you very much, very much, very much.
Jesus loves you very much. Yes, Jesus loves you.**

Play this active game with your child: **Say: Who does *Jesus* love? *Jesus* loves you when you clap.** (*Clap your hands.*) **Jesus loves you when you crawl.** (*Crawl around.*) **Jesus loves you when you walk.** (*Walk around.*) **Jesus loves you when you fall down.** (*Fall down with child.*) **Jesus loves you!** (*Pick up baby and cuddle.*)

Read the book *Jesus Is My Friend* with your baby or woddler. (This board book is published by Abingdon Press and is available in Christian bookstores.) Point to *Jesus* in the pictures. Use other Bible storybooks with your child and point out *Jesus* in them as well.

Because it is August, it may be hot. Take your baby or woddler outside and let him or her take joy in the warmth of the world that God created. **Say: God made the world. *Jesus* is God's Son.** Sprinkle water on your baby's legs and feet as well as on your own. **Say: Water is something we need in God's world. *Jesus* drank water. God made water.**

Another fun activity is to spread a piece of blue fabric on the ground or on a floor. **Say: This is a lake. *Jesus* often went to Lake Galilee.** Spread out some blocks on the blue fabric and tell the child that they are boats and fish. Play with your child and enjoy using your imagination!

Tell your child that she or he lives in a family. Talk and point to the individual people in your family. Point to Daddy and **say: That is Daddy. He loves you.** Point to yourself and **say: I am Mommy. I love you. *Jesus* lived in a family, too. He had a mother and a father. He had sisters and brothers.** Point to photographs of your family members. Say their names to your baby or woddler and **say:** *(Person's name)* **loves you. *Jesus* loves you. God loves you. You are loved!**

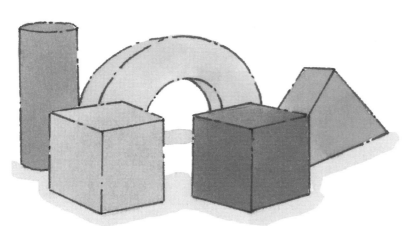

PRAYER

Lord,
Thank you for this little one given from above.
May your loving hands work through mine to
show this child your love.

PRAISE

Eyes and Ears Praise
(to the tune of "London Bridge")

God gave you two EYES to see,
Eyes to see, eyes to see.
God gave you two eyes to see.
What do you see?
(Pause to talk about what you can see.)

God gave you two EARS to hear,
Ears to hear, ears to hear.
God gave you two
ears to hear.
What do you
hear?
*(Pause to talk
about what you
hear.)*

God gave you two HANDS to clap,
Hands to clap, hands to clap.
God gave you two hands to clap
your praise to God!
*(Guide the child in simple hand-clapping
during this verse.)*

God gave you a MOUTH to sing,
Mouth to sing, mouth to sing.
God gave you a mouth to sing your thanks
to God!
*(Point to own mouth and help the child discover
her or his mouth.)*

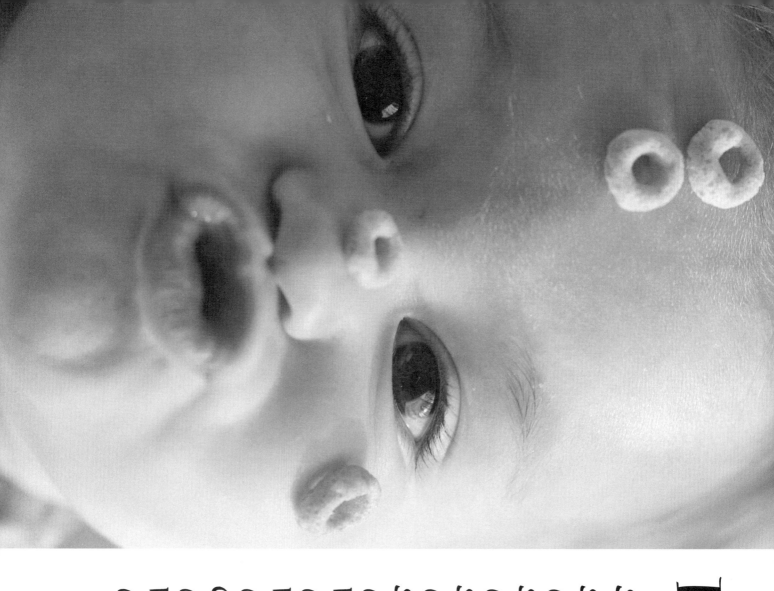

PLAY

Sticky Snacks
Sticky fingers,
(Wiggle your fingers.)
Sticky toes,
(Wiggle child's toes.)
Sticky snacks
(Tap fingertips on thumb.)
Stuck on my nose.
(Point to nose.)
Wash my fingers.
(Rub hands together.)
Wash my toes.
(Wipe off child's toes.)
Clean me up, and
(Rub cheeks with hands.)
Watch me grow.
(Stretch arms high in the air.)